D0571662

I◆I

THE CONSTITUTION

I◆I

■■■■|||| *American Government*

The Constitution

George H. Jenkins

The Rourke Corporation, Inc.

The Rourke Corporation, Inc.
P.O. Box 3328, Vero Beach, FL 32964

Jenkins, George H., 1950-
    The Constitution / by George H. Jenkins.
        p.   cm. — (American government)
    Includes bibliographical references and index.
        Summary: Discusses the origin and drafting of the Constitution and gives an article-by-article explanation of its provisions.
        ISBN 0-86593-085-6
        1. United States—Constitutional law—Juvenile literature.   2. United States—Constitutional history—Juvenile literature.   [1. United States—Constitutional law. 2. United States—Constitutional history.]   I. Title.   II. Series.
    KF4550.Z9J44   1990
    342.73'029—dc20   90-38803
    [347.30229]   CIP
                                                                                      AC

Series Editor: Gregory Lee
Editors: Elizabeth Sirimarco, Marguerite Aronowitz
Book design and production: The Creative Spark,
 Capistrano Beach, CA
Cover photograph: Jon Feingersh/Tom Stack & Associates

Authors' Note

All descriptions of the workings of the American Government that appear in this book are authentic, as are the citations of historical figures and events. Only the characters who carry the story line are fictional.

Table of Contents

1

Revolutionary Beginnings

Maria Chase watched as her classroom at Redmond Adult Community Center filled up with new students. Maria was a teacher in political science at a nearby junior college, but two nights a week she taught a class on the Constitution to immigrants studying for their United States citizenship. Usually, these adult students were not eager to spend their evenings learning about a 200-year-old piece of paper, but she would soon try to change their minds.

Maria listened to the murmuring discontent as the class discussed among themselves the evening's prospect of boredom. This reaction was not new to Maria, but it saddened her to think that most people were reluctant to hear about the Constitution of their adopted country. When they finished her class, however, and when they became naturalized citizens, they would know more about the history of the United States government than many of those who were born here!

The class settled down and was waiting for Maria to begin. She glanced from face to face, enjoying her game of guessing the origin of each student. Many of the faces were older than hers, some carved with weary lines from a life in another country. She had her hands full. Experience had taught her that an older class would probably challenge everything she said.

Independence Hall in Philadelphia was where the Declaration of Independence was signed, notifying the English government that the colonies were "free and independent states."

"Good evening all," Maria began, "I am Maria Chase. I was born in Spain and, like yourselves, I once attended a course like this to qualify for citizenship. I'd like to begin by asking you to please tell the class your name, the country where you were born, and what you know about the Constitution of the United States."

Everyone either looked down at their desk or around the room to see if anyone was volunteering. No one wanted to be the first to speak. A dark-haired woman with bright golden hoop earrings started things off.

"My name is Evita Diego, and I was born in Sao Paulo, Brazil. I'm afraid I do not know too much about your Constitution, that is why I am here."

Soon other members of the class began offering their ideas. Maria was not surprised that their thoughts about the Constitution were varied. Some correctly referred to it as the "Supreme Law of the Land," but had little understanding of what that meant. Others thought the document was the "source" of all American rights.

"Most of your views on this subject are pretty good for a start," said Maria. "For the next few weeks we're going to sort them out and give you some idea of what it was like during the time the Constitution was written. The wording in the Constitution was carefully chosen. We'll explain why the men who wrote this document were so careful about their choice of words, and the importance of those words to all of us in this room."

Why Is The Constitution Important?

"A question please," voiced a tall gentleman in the last row.

"Yes?" Maria said.

"My name is Karl Borman, and I came from East Germany before the Berlin Wall was torn down. Life was not easy there when I fled my country. I don't wish to appear ungrateful to my new country, but...." Karl paused.

"Karl, please say what's on your mind. You're among friends, and disagreeing with authority—me, for instance—is a favorite American pastime."

Karl blushed and waited for the laughter to stop. "Thank you," he went on. "I don't see how taking a law class on the Constitution will help. I don't intend to become a lawyer. Also, what is so important about how the document was written? Are not 'constitutional issues' of interest only to high judges and expensive lawyers?"

"First of all," Maria began gently, "this is not a 'law class' on the Constitution. What we'll be doing is getting an overview of the Constitution, and a glimpse at the times in American history that produced it. You could say the Constitution is the 'blueprint' for our gov-

Ratification Of The Constitution

On September 17, 1787, the Constitution was adopted by the Convention of the States. Ratification occurred among the individual states in order as follows:

DELAWARE, December 7, 1787. Yeas 30 (unanimous).

PENNSYLVANIA, December 12, 1787. Yeas 46; Nays 23.

NEW JERSEY, December 18, 1787. Yeas 38 (unanimous).

GEORGIA, January 2, 1788. Yeas 26 (unanimous).

CONNECTICUT, January 9, 1788. Yeas 128; Nays 40.

MASSACHUSETTS, February 6, 1788. Yeas 187; Nays 168.

MARYLAND, April 28, 1788. Yeas 63; Nays 11.

SOUTH CAROLINA, May 23, 1788. Yeas 149; Nays 73.

NEW HAMPSHIRE, June 21, 1788. Yeas 57; Nays 46.

VIRGINIA, June 25, 1788. Yeas 89; Nays 79.

NEW YORK, July 26, 1788. Yeas 30; Nays 27.

NORTH CAROLINA, November 21, 1789. Yeas 184; Nays 77.

RHODE ISLAND, May 29, 1790. Yeas 34; Nays 32.

The signing of the United States Constitution is often depicted as a joyous, unanimous ritual. In fact, the battle for ratification was a prolonged and vigorous one, and it took more than two years for all the colonies to approve.

ernment—when you understand it, you'll be able to appreciate becoming a citizen and the privilege of voting.

"Second, you will find that the Constitution has a direct impact on all of us and how we live. For instance, as Karl just learned, to challenge authority is your right as an American.

"The framers of the Constitution thought a lot about the need to protect human rights. Although they couldn't anticipate the kinds of problems we are faced with today, they did decide on how 'government by the people' should operate and, through our elected officials, find ways to solve potential problems."

Maria paused for a moment to let that sink in, then said, "Okay, class, feel free to interrupt with questions at any time. Tonight we'll start at the beginning—the American Revolution."

Seeds Of Revolution

Maria began by painting a picture of the lives of many who struggled to build up the original 13 colonies.

Prior to the Revolutionary War, Maria began, most of the colonists referred to themselves as Englishmen, or subjects of the English king, George III. At that time, the American colonies had assemblies for governing. The king allowed the control of local matters by the American colonists under the watchful eye of his personal representatives, who saw that English law was enforced in all matters.

Eventually, however, the colonists began to note certain differences between English law for Englishmen and English law for the colonists. Things were simply not the same for the colonists as they were for their brothers in England.

American Englishmen began to protest these differences vigorously, but they were ignored. The reason for this was simple: the colonies did not have any direct representation in the British parliament or influence with the king.

Rights and freedoms enjoyed by the English and protected by their courts and laws were often ignored when it came to the American colonists, who expected the same treatment.

"A double standard," said a woman named Dolores from Peru. "Is that how you say it?"

"Exactly," Maria replied, glad that her students were getting the point.

As the colonial population grew, and another generation was being born in the colonies, many began thinking of themselves as American instead of English.

By the mid-1700s, life was getting to be frustrating for the colonists. Americans were being taxed without their consent. Imports to the colonies had to travel through British ports, giving an unfair advantage to English merchants. English troops were sometimes housed in American homes without the owner's consent. Local legislatures were abolished for passing laws contrary to the will of the English Crown.

"These grievances were not simple issues," Maria explained. "They were as complex as the many social issues that concern us today."

"Did all colonial Americans support the revolution?" asked one Nigerian student named Robert.

Maria explained that the colonial population was divided into three segments: those who supported the Crown (called Tories), those who were neutral, and those in rebellion—who called themselves "patriots."

"To be a rebel in those times must have been very dangerous," observed a pupil from Pakistan named Mohammed. Other students nodded, and Maria agreed.

In fact, the grievances became so numerous that eventually the colonies decided some action needed to be taken. On September 4, 1774, the First Continental Congress was formed in Philadelphia in order to represent American interests to the English Crown. This congress issued a "Declaration of Rights," and went on record as planning to boycott goods from England. This first congress was not a true government, but only acted to convey the will of the 13 "sovereign" or independent colonies.

"The results of this first congress didn't amount to much," said Maria, "but the final straw was the outbreak of violence at Lexington, Massachusetts on April 19, 1775. Have any of you heard of the 'shot heard round the world'? The colonies were most definitely in rebellion, and the British were determined to punish their naughty child."

On May 10, 1775, a Second Continental Congress was formed. This congress acted more like a government because it established the Continental Army and issued Continental money. It also sought a last chance for peace with England by drawing up a document called the "Olive Branch Petition," but the Crown rejected it, and the War of Independence was on.

The Declaration Of Independence

The unjust treatment of English subjects in America by King George III had now reached a point of no return. On July 2, 1776, the congressional delegates approved a declaration of independence, and on July 4 the final draft was passed by 12 of the 13 colonies. John Hancock, president of the Congress, signed the document, and it was witnessed by secretary Charles Thomson. The familiar 56 signatures were added later, on August 2, to a newly printed copy.

Maria paused to accept a question. "I am Henri Rene from Gruisson, France. I think the story of your independence is—how do you say—very moving. But I don't understand how is this Declaration of Independence related to the Constitution?"

Maria smiled and explained.

"The Declaration of Independence did more than inform King George that the colonies would no longer obey his laws. It announced to the world that the colonies were now and forever independent states, and that they were entitled to be taken seriously in world affairs. The French were among the first to recognize our declaration and support our revolution, because they were constantly at war with England and this was a great way to strike a blow at the English."

The Declaration also helped at home. Many "fence-sitters"—the neutral Americans—now sided with the patriotic cause. They got "caught up" in the excitement. Even in England there was much sympathy in support of the colonies, which caused the government difficulty at home. The Declaration had listed for all the world to see formal charges of tyrannical acts committed by King George's government against his own people.

"The document formally established the political concepts that found their way into the Constitution, including the belief that all men are created equal, that government governs only with the consent of the people, and that everyone's rights are *inalienable* (one is born with rights, and no government can deprive a person of them). The founders attributed these rights to God, but whatever one's religious beliefs, his or her rights are that person's rights without question. Human beings automatically have certain rights.

"And," Maria concluded, "I think that's all we have time for tonight."

2

The Articles Of Confederation

During their next class session, Maria was ready to take her students into a subject that confused many Americans: the first attempt by the founders to form a government.

"Good evening, class," she began. "How is everyone tonight?" This time the faces in the class were smiling as they voiced eager hellos. "Let's start by talking about the Articles of Confederation."

"The Confederacy?" said Joaquin, a coffee merchant from Venezuela. "I thought that was in your civil war period."

"No, Joaquin, I don't mean that Confederacy, I mean the first government formed by the 13 colonies—they wanted to be a confederation too, and so they wrote some articles that defined how they would work together. Fortunately for us they didn't work, so later we got our Constitution."

In time the colonists realized that their original Continental congresses were no substitute for a national government. Some Americans believed in a strong, central government, while others supported a national identity for each state. The "confederacy" would link the states only in matters that affected them all.

The power of the early congresses was kept deliberately weak by the states. "National" government meant the creation of a new nation from the 13 colonies, and a strong central government was felt by

This Ethiopian family represents yet another generation of immigrants who have come to America to enjoy the freedoms protected by the Constitution.

some to be just what the colonies were fighting against. This fear of central authority prevailed when the first government of the United States was created in the Articles of Confederation.

Fighting Over Words

Eight days after the signing of the Declaration of Independence, John Dickenson authored and presented to the Second Continental Congress the first draft of the "Articles of Confederation and Perpetual Union." Dickenson was chairman of a 13-man committee that was asked to present a suitable charter, or plan, for a central government. But the original draft was soon torn apart because it called for a much stronger government than most of the delegates to the Continental Congress had in mind.

The need for the Articles would not go away. Since each state was acting like an independent country, problems between the states and the Continental Congress grew worse. Trade wars erupted between states. For example, a farmer in New Jersey could not sell his goods in New York without being heavily taxed. And many states simply would not pay their fair share of the cost of the War of Independence.

Heads of state from other nations often received representatives from different states *and* the Continental Congress, which confused them as to who was really in charge.

The draft of the Articles of Confederation was finally adopted on November 13, 1777, thanks to the efforts of a newcomer to Congress, Dr. Thomas Burke. Dr. Burke put an end to the arguments about "national" versus "continental" power by suggesting that the states should determine the specific powers of the national government, and reserve all other powers to themselves.

Thus the country's first national constitution came to consist of 13 articles. The first article gave the nation an official name: "The United States of America."

The remaining articles outlined the makeup of the Confederation Congress of the United States—still the only government body—and its powers. Included were the following: Congress could declare war; make treaties and alliances with other nations; settle boundary disputes between two or more states; and borrow money. Also included were specifics about what the Confederation Congress could not do, including regulating interstate trade and collecting taxes.

On March 1, 1781, six years after the Revolutionary War began and several months before its end at Yorktown, Virginia, the Congress met at the Philadelphia home of the president of the Congress, Samuel Huntington. On that day, Maryland became the last state to ratify the Articles of Confederation and Perpetual Union, and a new government was born. Samuel Huntington was really the first president of the "United States of America."

A Poor And Powerless Confederation

"So what is so important about this Confederation?" asked Emilio, a man from Mexico.

"Well," replied Maria, "the founders couldn't have known that the Confederation was going to be unworkable until it was tried. The weak results of the Confederation helped the authors of the Constitution write a better blueprint for things to come. So the Articles of Confederation are of interest because they show us that the founders were human—they didn't get it right the first time.

"Some men, like James Madison, recognized several weaknesses in the new charter. He knew that in order for the United States to survive in a hostile world, the national government needed to be granted certain powers.

"For example, the Congress could ask the states for funds to carry out national business, yet nowhere could Madison find where it said that the Congress could make the states pay. In other words, the Confederation had no power to enforce its own laws. In another case, Congress could not settle trade disputes between states because it was specifically prohibited from regulating interstate trade. Congress also couldn't raise taxes, and that meant trouble keeping the Continental Army together."

Maria then gave her class one example of how close the United States came to be without any defense.

In January 1783, restless Army officers sent Major Alexander McDougal to Philadelphia with a petition to Congress. The soldiers of the Continental Army, unpaid and underfed, were demanding their wages. The petition demanded that Congress pay the soldiers at once. Unfortunately, this was a demand the Congress could not meet.

Rumors spread about a possible march on Philadelphia, or even total abandonment of the states by the Army. It was even said that the soldiers would take their families and form a new nation in the west. Only a last-minute, personal plea from General Washington himself to his officers kept them from rebelling.

Foreign policy was a mess as well. The Spanish, who occupied what is now part of the southern United States, refused to allow

James Madison, fourth president of the United States, was one of the principal architects of the Constitution. Madison argued strenuously for ratification of the Constitution through The Federalist Papers.

Americans access to the lower Mississippi River, a route vital to western American trade. But again, the Confederate Congress was powerless to negotiate a peaceful compromise.

The new government failed economically because it could not raise taxes to fund its own operation. It also failed to enforce its own laws because it had no executive branch to enforce those laws. And even if it could enforce the law, there was no judicial branch of government to provide judges to try cases.

As the Revolutionary War drew to a close and the United States struggled to gain a place in the world of nations, the states drifted even further apart. In light of all the difficulties being experienced by this fledgling nation, even opponents of the idea of central government began to see that something had to be done. Finally, a constitutional convention was called for May 1787, where the job of the state delegations would be to fix the problems of the Confederation.

"But the men who showed up had something pretty radical in mind," Maria told her class. "Some didn't know it yet, but these men were about to write the most important document in democratic history."

3

The Federal Convention

"Please Ms. Chase," asked Miyoshi Tanaka, "where was the Constitution written?"

"In Philadelphia, home of the Liberty Bell. I'm sure you've seen pictures of it with its famous crack," answered Maria. "Several state delegations attended this convention, and their purpose was to revise the existing Articles of Confederation, not to start from scratch and write a new document."

Two distinct views began to emerge in Philadelphia. On one side were the *Federalists*, who supported a much stronger central government. Opposing them were the *Anti-Federalists*, who felt the existing Articles could be amended or changed to correct earlier shortcomings, and still protect the rights of the states. There were many other issues dividing the two political camps, but the most important issue debated was the old fear of a too powerful central government.

The Anti-Federalists maintained that the states were like separate, small countries. To illustrate this, when William Houston of Georgia traveled to New York, he wrote that he was leaving "my country to go to a strange land amongst strangers." Just the problem of distance had a great impact on this debate. No matter where the capital of a new central government might be located, it would still be too far away for some of the states. And many colonists were suspicious of being ruled from a distance—they had just freed themselves from one such government.

"The Federalists knew that popular support would lean toward the Anti-Federalists, and so they proposed a constitutional convention," Maria said. "Public prejudice toward a new government had to be dealt with. The public reason for this convention was to *amend* (or modify) the existing Articles of Confederation, but the private intention of the Federalists was to create an entirely new government."

On May 25, 1787, George Washington was elected President of the Convention. Although retired from public life, Washington was pressured to accept the post because his participation was considered essential. Because of Washington's tremendous popularity, the public would be more inclined to accept the results of the convention.

On May 29, the delegates voted to keep the proceedings of the convention absolutely secret. There were several reasons for this. First, the delegates did not want to alarm the public in the middle of a debate whose outcome was unknown. Second, it was felt that members would speak more openly if their views were not open to the public, possibly to be ridiculed. Finally, and most important, the delegates wanted the results of their effort—whatever the outcome—to stand on their own merits before the people. In other words, the product of the convention would be judged by the people without their knowing the arguments, disagreements, and compromises that went into producing this sensitive document.

The members were very serious about secrecy. They were so serious that detailed accounts of the actual debates as recorded by James Madison were not made public until 50 years later.

The convention got off to a hot start. The same day the secrecy issue was voted on, the Virginia delegation opened the debate by submitting 15 resolutions, later known as the "Virginia Plan." The first acknowledged the stated purpose of the convention: "[T]he Articles of Confederation ought to be so corrected and enlarged as to accomplish the objects proposed by their institution, namely common defence, security of liberty, and general welfare." This first Virginia resolution was immediately agreed upon. After all, it stated plainly the goal of the convention.

On May 30, the delegates came to a major decision that signaled the beginning of the end of the first government of the United States. They adopted the third of the Virginia resolutions, which stated that "a national government ought to be established, consisting of a supreme legislative, executive, and judiciary."

By adopting the third Virginia resolution to modify the Articles, the delegates had formally changed the purpose of the convention.

The Three-Branch Proposal

"Does anyone know what we mean by 'checks and balances'?" Maria asked her class. No one answered. "It means that no single branch of government is senior to another. We have a three-branch system: executive, legislative, and judicial. This system appealed to the delegates because it reinforced their belief that people tend to be corrupted by power."

Through proposal and counterproposal, the delegates slowly and carefully shaped and formed the new government. Compromise was an important and necessary attitude at the convention. Compromise established the *bicameral* or "two-chambered" legislature. Compromise also settled the great issue of equal representation between the small and large states. The "Great Compromise," proposed by Roger Sherman of Connecticut, would give all states an equal vote in the Senate, but the population of each state would determine the number of votes in the House of Representatives. Compromise created an Executive branch headed by a single president. And finally, compromise produced the Supreme Court as final judge in disputes.

At the end of the convention, the delegates decided that the new Constitution would take effect when it was ratified by at least nine of the 13 states.

The creation of the Constitution of the United States is often referred to as "the miracle at Philadelphia." Different people from different backgrounds came together during the hot days of spring and summer to meld together their beliefs and differences. They established a single document of law that would be the basis of the

The checks and balances of the Constitution were evident during the "flag-burning" controversy of 1989-90, the result of a Supreme Court ruling that stated mistreatment of the flag was a protected form of free expression under the First Amendment. Congress passed a law to override the judicial branch decision, but lost again when the Supreme Court overturned the new federal law.

most successful democracy in the world. It was an awesome event.

The Federal Convention closed on September 17, 1787, with the signing of the Constitution. Three of the delegates, however, George Mason, Edmund Randolph, and Elbridge Gerry, refused to sign it because it did not contain a specific list of rights of the people.

The Fight For Ratification

The Federal Convention had conducted its work, business, and debates in total secrecy for four months. Now came the difficult part. The delegates returned home. Their new Constitution and the government it would create had to be sold to each of the states and its people. Every state had to establish a ratifying convention, select delegates, and debate the merits of the Constitution.

First the people had to be informed about the contents of the document they were being asked to ratify (approve). Newspapers printed copies of the wording. Private printers were hired to print and distribute leaflet copies to those who could read, especially the land owners. As the people became aware of what was written at the Convention, great debates once again began sweeping through the 13 states.

During the critical period from late 1787 to early 1788, a famous debate that became known as the Ratifications Contest took place between the Federalists and the Anti-Federalists. Three men—Alexander Hamilton, James Madison, and John Jay—wrote and published a series of essays in support of the new Constitution. These essays were collected in a single volume and later became known as the *Federalist Papers*. Patrick Henry and John DeWitt, noted Anti-Federalists, argued against the new Constitution in the Philadelphia and New York papers. This collection of essays became known as the *Anti-Federalist* papers.

The first state to ratify the Constitution was Delaware, with a unanimous vote of its delegates on December 7, 1787. The first big ratification fight was in Massachusetts, where a stirring and heated debate finally ended with the vote narrowly approving the new Constitution.

But the Virginia convention provided the most intense debates. Patrick Henry and James Madison faced each other in fierce one-on-one arguments. Virginia became the tenth state to ratify on June 25, 1788.

The last state to accept the new Constitution was Rhode Island, which ratified the document on May 29, 1790. This came about after the new government had already been installed and George Washington was sworn in as its new president.

The Bill Of Rights

"What about the Bill of Rights?" asked Juanita from Colombia.

"You're one jump ahead of me," Maria smiled. "Actually, the first act of the new government was to have the Congress draft and submit a bill of rights."

The Anti-Federalists were not happy that the new Constitution didn't spell out the rights of the people in specific terms, so a promise was made to the Anti-Federalists—specifically in New York and Virginia—that this issue would be resolved at a later date. Both states ratified the Constitution only on condition that a bill of rights would be amended to the Constitution.

Debates in Congress over the amendments lasted more than three-and-one-half months. James Madison wrote and submitted eight amendments, and two more were added to protect rights not specifically mentioned in Madison's original eight.

This effort was an act of good faith by the new government to assure its people that the original principles and rights listed in the Declaration of Independence were officially incorporated into the Constitution. The Bill of Rights was ratified by all 13 states, and became the first ten amendments to the Constitution in December 1791.

The Preamble

Maria glanced about the room at the faces of her students. They all looked impressed at the amount of effort it took to create the Constitution.

"The document itself seems so simple today," said Joaquin.

"The real effort is in understanding and keeping it," Maria replied. "Many schoolchildren in America are required to memorize the preamble to the Constitution, but I wonder how many adults in America understand what those few words really mean." To illustrate

Women weren't specifically excluded from participating in politics by the Constitution—it was just taken for granted that concern with government was not a proper role for women.

her point, Maria recited the preamble from memory.

"*"We the People of the United States, in order to form a more perfect union, establish justice, insure domestic tranquility, provide for the common defense, promote the general welfare, and secure the blessings of liberty to ourselves and our posterity, do ordain and establish this Constitution for the United States of America.'*"

Then Maria began to interpret what she had just said. "'We the people' means that the citizens were already united, under the Articles of Confederation, but that they desired to form a better government. The founders were admitting to the world that they didn't do so well the first time, and were trying to improve the second time around.

"Then there is the list of objectives, or reasons, why they wanted to create this more perfect union—like 'justice,' for instance, or 'common defense.' 'Promote the general welfare' can be interpreted as what government does today: enacting laws that most of us feel are important such as social security or the Superfund environmental clean-up process.

"Finally, the preamble tells us what was being done: 'establish this Constitution for the United States of America.' Because of the will of the people, the Constitution created a new sovereign state, and set forth its framework.

"By writing the Constitution, the founders created a new class of citizen called the *citizen-constituent*. The citizens are therefore the holders of the power behind the Constitution.

"This is quite important," Maria emphasized. "What citizens holding power means is that we are ultimately responsible for the conduct of our government and the impact it has on our lives. For example, if you have a particular social issue you consider important, you can bring it to the people for action."

4

The Branch Of Lawmakers

In the next class Maria began exploring the separate articles of the Constitution and how they outlined an entirely new system of government—the first of its kind in the history of man.

"The original Constitution is divided into seven articles, or sections, that outline the powers and restrictions of our government. You may think this is just bureaucratic paperwork, but the founders argued vigorously over every detail—every word—because of their fear of tyranny. It's been over 200 years, and the Constitution is proof that while it's not perfect, it has certainly kept America a democracy."

She pointed to the chalkboard where "Article I" was written above a simple diagram of the two houses that make up Congress.

Article I created and defined the powers of the Congress, which is a bicameral or two-house legislature consisting of the Senate and the House of Representatives. This two-house principle was an important compromise that solved the "equal representation" arguments during the constitutional convention. Small states had been fearful of representation that was based upon population, where they would have little voice because of their limited number of residents. Now they are "equal" in the Senate, because each state has the same

The legislative branch of government are the two houses of Congress, the Senate and the House of Representatives. Both meet during two lengthy sessions per year in the Capitol Building.

number of senators: two. In the House of Representatives, however, each state has the number of representatives proportional to its population. So New York and California have many, while Idaho and Rhode Island have few. But neither house can dominate the other, because both houses and the president must approve a bill before it can become law.

"This arrangement was probably the single most important compromise in the whole package," Maria stated.

The House Of Representatives

Members of the House of Representatives are "chosen every second year by the people of the several states." Convention delegate Elbridge Gerry of Massachusetts argued for annual elections, saying that electing representatives each year was "the only defense against tyranny." But his point of view was thought to be a bit extreme.

"Would you like to know the requirements?" Maria asked. "You will all be able to qualify one day, so you might want to write this down. Members of the House must be at least 25 years old, have been a citizen for at least seven years and, when elected, be 'an inhabitant of the State in which he shall be chosen.'

"Notice that the qualifications for members uses the word 'person,' which means that women were never really denied office by the Constitution, but the use of the pronoun 'he' was certainly an indication of the times. Women were not even allowed to vote, much less run for office. When Jeannette Rankin of Montana became the first woman to sit in the House in 1917, it was the result of slowly changing social attitudes. And this success by an American woman was obtained three years before women were guaranteed the right to vote!"

Maria explained that the section dealing with the "apportionment of representatives and of direct taxes" was changed by the 14th Amendment, because at the time the Constitution was written, slavery was a major issue. Since each state was taxed by the number of people living in the state, the status of slaves first had to be resolved.

In the compromise that followed, free persons, including those "bound to service" (in essence, slaves for a limited time) counted as whole persons for purposes of taxation. Native American Indians "not taxed" were excluded from a state's population, and slaves were counted as three-fifths of a person under the umbrella term "all other persons." So the fact that slavery existed was acknowledged by the founders, although the practice itself is not mentioned by name in the Constitution. The 14th Amendment later removed any reference to partial persons and simply used the phrase, "male voters 21 years of age" to define representation.

Maria could see the looks of bewilderment in her class. "We'll talk about slavery and women's rights on another night. But right now, let's stay with the document and what it means. How are the number of representatives for each state determined? The rate is 'one for each thirty thousand' persons. Originally the figure was 40,000, but George Washington argued that the figure was too high. He suggested 30,000 to provide a higher percentage of representatives per person.

"As the United States population grew, so did the House of Representatives. In 1929, the number of Representatives was limited to 435, so today each member represents approximately half a million citizens. If the original 1-to-30,000 ratio were still intact, the House would have more than 7,000 members!

"Can anyone tell me," Maria asked, "what would happen if a large portion of the population shifted from one state to another?" Evita raised her hand. "Would the seats of the House change so that the state that has more in population would get more seats?"

"Right," Maria said, "and the opposite would also be true. If a state loses population, the number of seats it holds in the House goes down. But every state must have at least one representative in the House."

It is possible that the numbers taken from the 1990 census will result in increased representatives from the so-called "Sun Belt" states of Texas and California, while the northern industrial states of New York and Illinois may suffer a loss. This is due to the recent migration of workers to the southwest that occurred during the 1980s. The process of assigning the seats is called "apportionment," and takes place following each ten-year census.

"I thought," said Karl, "that the process is called 'redistricting.'"

"Yes, partially, since redistricting is the second half of the process."

After the census counts are in and Congress has adjusted the seating by state, each state must draw up new internal boundaries to represent their congressional districts. Since this is done by each state's legislature, the party in power has the advantage of drawing boundaries that favor its own members (called *gerrymandering*). This privilege of a ruling party has long been a source of conflict because it influences—some say unfairly—how the ruling party stays in power. So the majority party at the state level can make sure it will retain or gain seats in the Congress following each census.

The Senate

Senators are elected to six-year terms, with one-third of the Senate's 100 members coming up for reelection every two years. The reason for six-year terms is so there will always be a group of experienced senators in office. A complete turnover of the Senate in one election is not possible. The founders believed this would give the government more stability.

Originally it was the responsibility of each state legislature to choose its two senators, but in 1913 the 17th Amendment was passed, turning over this power of electing senators to the people of each state.

The president used to have the privilege of appointing a new senator to serve out a vacant term (due to resignation, illness or death). In 1917, however, this power was given to the governor of each state, keeping the selection of its senators in the state's hands.

Senators must be at least 30 years old and residents of the state they represent. The must also have been United States citizens for nine years. Two senators have been challenged over these restrictions, including Senator-elect Albert Gallatin who was barred from assuming office in 1793 because he allegedly was not a citizen for nine years. Senator Henry Clay was underage when elected, but was allowed to serve because he reached the minimum age prior to being sworn into office.

The vice president serves as president of the Senate, where he conducts its day-to-day sessions. He can vote on laws and resolutions only when there is a tie. In practice, the vice president rarely attends Senate sessions. The tie-breaking vote, however, gives vice presidents the opportunity to support their party in a dramatic way. Many important issues have been carried by this single vote when the senators were divided along party lines.

The "republican" form of government outlined in the Constitution allows all citizens to vote for representatives, who then make laws on their behalf in the state legislatures and in the Congress.

Other Congressional Duties

The House of Representatives has the sole power of *impeachment*, the right to "bring to trial" elected officials or judges who have violated their oath of office. To date the House has "impeached" 15 government officials, including President Andrew Johnson (acquitted by the Senate in 1868), and Supreme Court Justice Samuel Chase (acquitted in 1805). President Richard Nixon became the first and only president to resign from office when the House Judiciary Committee voted to open impeachment proceedings in 1974.

The Constitution spells out the rules for conducting an impeachment trial. First, the House votes for impeachment, then the Senate tries the case and serves as the jury. If the president is being tried, the Chief Justice of the Supreme Court presides instead of the vice president. Impeachment leads to removal from office, but does not exempt the impeached official from criminal prosecution later.

One of the most hotly-debated constitutional mandates at the Philadelphia convention was that Congress meet "at least once each year." Some thought this was too often. Said Massachusetts delegate Rufus King, "Too much legislating [is] a great vice." Travel in those days was also a factor, keeping these men away from their families for long periods of time.

Rules for conducting daily business in Congress are also listed in Article I, as is the requirement that each house publish a public record of its legislative activity. This was considered to be extremely important. James Wilson, a delegate from Pennsylvania, insisted that the people had a "right to know what their agents are doing or have done." Despite this rule, however, the Senate met for the first five years of its existence behind closed doors, using a "secrecy" clause in Article I that provided a loophole. Today the proceedings of each house are published together in the *Congressional Record* that's available to anyone.

The Constitution requires that members of Congress be paid for their services in an amount "to be ascertained by law." What this means is that Congress can set the amount of its own wages. This fact has been a continuous source of argument. James Madison stated that it "was an indecent thing and might, in time, prove…dangerous." Even today a public outcry is heard whenever members of Congress try to give themselves a pay raise.

Congressional Power

The last three sections of Article I reflect the founders' concern about governmental powers. The Constitution defines all powers granted to Congress as a whole. It also expressly denies or prohibits certain actions.

The listing of these congressional powers takes up 18 short paragraphs. The first 17 are called the "enumerated powers" (meaning powers that are specifically explained), and the final paragraph is the famous "elastic clause." Many congressional powers that have emerged over the years are based on the "implied powers" granted by this section.

Powers granted to Congress include the right to raise money through taxes and duties, and the right to borrow money. All taxes or fees are supposed to be "uniform throughout the United States."

Other powers granted to Congress include:

- Regulating international trade, interstate commerce and immigration
- Coining money and regulating its value
- Establishing post offices and federal court districts
- Creating patent and copyright laws
- Raising and supporting the armed forces
- Declaring war

The final elastic clause was little noticed when enacted, but it since has opened the door to an enormous increase in federal power. Congress may "make all laws which shall be necessary and proper for carrying into execution the foregoing powers." This is an open-ended clause that has led to the creation of a vast government bureaucracy that regulates and enforces federal laws throughout the United States.

Powers Denied

One of Congress' most important no-nos is that "the privilege of the writ of *habeas corpus* shall not be suspended." What does this mean? If the government accuses someone of breaking the law, it must give that individual his or her day in court right away to determine whether there was just cause for arrest.

During the Civil War, this clause was suspended by Abraham Lincoln. The Constitution states that it cannot be suspended except in times of "rebellion," so Lincoln put that exception to the test. The government could now detain anyone for any reason. This violation was justified by supporters of Lincoln as being necessary due to the state of war between the states.

The class looked confused, so it was time for a practical example. "There's another excellent clause that protects you from being charged with a crime that's not yet a crime," said Maria.

"Say again please?" asked Miyoshi as she scribbled notes.

"I'll read it," said Maria. "'No bill of attainder or *ex post facto* law shall be passed.' Ex post facto is a Latin term meaning 'after the fact.' In other words, you cannot violate some future law and have the government prosecute you. Think of it this way: you can't be brought to court for eating your lunch on the steps of the Capitol on June 6 if the law prohibiting eating your lunch there doesn't go into effect until June 7." The class laughed.

"Go ahead, laugh—the founders knew that many repressive governments did do such things. But there's one thing that Congress can do now that it originally could not do, and that's tax all your incomes." The class booed, then broke out laughing again.

"With the passage of the 16th Amendment, Congress obtained the power to tax your income directly."

Maria then wrapped up the evening by outlining the remainder of the limitations imposed upon the federal government, including:

- No preference shall be given in the regulation of commerce
- No money shall be drawn from the treasury without a full public accounting

- No title of nobility can be granted by the United States. An individual may accept the honor of a title from a foreign nation, but only with the consent of the Congress.

Powers prohibited to the states are, in effect, powers granted to the federal government. States may not enter treaties, coin money, pass ex post facto laws, give someone a title of nobility, and so forth.

"That's it for tonight!" Maria concluded. "Next week we'll discuss the presidency."

5

The Branch Of The Executive

There was a full house for the next Redmond Continuing Education class on the Constitution. Maria was going to talk about the executive branch of the government, the topic that most interested her students. After all, the president is the most visible and symbolic of the three branches of government.

Article II of the Constitution established the executive branch of the government by providing for a president, as chief executive, a vice president, and other subordinate officials. It also defines the qualifications for office, the manner of elections, and the powers and duties vested in these offices.

The president and vice president are elected to office by the vote of a body of electors, commonly called the Electoral College. These electors are selected by each of the state legislatures, who can have as many as the state has senators and representatives. But no senator or representative may serve as an elector.

As originally written, the Constitution established an elaborate method of determining who was elected to the office of president or vice president. But this method was replaced by the 12th Amendment to the Constitution. This amendment improved the process by making clear the exact step-by-step electoral method whereby the president and vice president are elected to office. The electoral process remains

The president is empowered by the Constitution to negotiate treaties with foreign powers. Here former President Ronald Reagan (left) signs a disarmament treaty with Soviet leader Mikhail Gorbachev.

in place today, although many people don't understand it and still believe that the popular vote elects these important people.

Robert interrupted. "You mean American citizens don't really elect the president?"

"Not directly. It's still possible for the popular vote to select one candidate for office and the Electoral College another. For example, Benjamin Harrison became president even though he lost the popular vote to Grover Cleveland. Harrison was elected to office by the Electoral College.

"The popular vote always influences state legislators, and is usually assumed to be binding. In other words, the smart state legislator responds to the will of the people. If the popular election is really close, however, we could see another president not popularly elected, like Benjamin Harrison. Many states do have laws that demand the winner of the popular election take all the state's electoral votes.

"Television voter projections and 'exit polls' have pretty much taken the suspense out of electing a president," Maria added.

"As most of you probably know, the president and vice president are elected together for a term of four years. After a presidential candidate is chosen at the convention, a vice presidential 'running mate' is named. He or she is always a member of the same party, right? Is that because of the law, do you think?"

Everyone looked at each other and shrugged. Nobody knew the answer.

"Well, guess what? Nothing in the Constitution says they both must be from the same party."

This created a stir. A young woman from England named Anne raised her hand. "Has there ever been a president from one party and a vice president from another?"

"Yes," Maria said. "In fact, when the nation was first created, *no* political parties existed! This meant that each candidate for office created his own support group to help him get elected. People who thought and felt alike about issues of the day formed parties to support candidates who felt the same way. As a result of this early way of doing things, the president and vice president often belonged to different political parties. A good example was John Adams, a member of the Federalist party, and his vice president, Thomas Jefferson, who belonged to a party called the Democratic-Republicans. Today's Democratic and Republican parties did not emerge until the mid-1800s."

Making It To The Top

The vice presidency has been regarded as a minor position throughout the history of the United States. With the exception of standing by to assume the duties of president, if necessary, the Constitution states that the vice president's principal job is to serve as the president of the Senate.

So poorly regarded has the status of the office of vice president been that one vice president, John N. Garner (1933-41), referred to the office as "hardly worth a pitcher of warm spit." More recently, however, presidents have begun enhancing the job of vice president by increasing the responsibilities of the post—most notably in diplomatic functions such as acting as emissary in foreign functions, and heading departmental efforts such as the space program and drug enforcement programs. The office of vice president is becoming more important with each administration.

To qualify to become president, you must be a natural-born citizen of the United States, 35 years old at the time of election, and a resident within the United States for at least 14 years. The youngest president elected was John F. Kennedy; the oldest Ronald Reagan. There are no other restrictions as to maximum age, gender, religion or race.

A vacancy in the office of the president due to death, resignation, or inability to discharge the powers and duties of the office, will result in the vice president taking over the presidency. This happened shortly after President Kennedy was assassinated, when Lyndon B. Johnson was sworn in as president on board Air Force One.

The Congress determines if the president or vice president is unable to fulfill the duties of office. Originally, the Constitution did not make it clear how Congress would determine if any member of the Executive branch was unable to fulfill the duties of office. The 25th Amendment, however, which deals with the conditions and situations for the transfer of power, made clear the responsibility of Congress.

The 25th Amendment also changed the clause of vacancy, which means that now the president can appoint a vice president, should that office become vacant. The amendment also clarifies and defines the conditions when the vice president may serve as "acting president," eventually giving power back to the president. These two provisions were first exercised when President Reagan voluntarily relinquished his power to then-Vice President George Bush because of impending surgery. When the president was well enough in a few days to assume his duties, Mr. Bush relinquished his authority as acting president.

The president is required by the Constitution to take the following oath or affirmation:

"I do solemnly swear (or affirm) that I will faithfully execute the office of President of the United States, and will to the best of my ability, preserve, protect and defend the Constitution of the United States."

Powers Of The President

The president is the commander in chief of all the armed forces, including any state militias when called to federal service. The president also has the power to grant reprieves and pardons for offenses against the United States, except in the case of impeachment.

Some of the president's powers are limited, however, as in making treaties with other nations. This also is true when he appoints ambassadors, judges, public ministers and consuls, department heads, and all other officers of the United States. These treaties and appointments must be made with a full two-thirds approval of the Senate.

The president's power to appoint Supreme Court justices has always been a political struggle, because political beliefs play a large role in choosing candidates. Supreme Court justices make the final interpretation over disputed matters that relate to the Constitution by interpreting what the Constitution says.

"Judicial interpretation of constitutional matters is difficult to understand," said Maria. "When a dispute needs to be settled and the issue or cause of the dispute is a constitutional one—such as the right to free speech or the right to worship as you please—the judge determines what the Constitution meant."

"They read minds, huh?" said Miyoshi.

"Well, no one can say with certainty what the founders would say about any one issue," replied Maria, "but that's what every justice tries to do.

"For instance, if you yell 'Fire!' in a crowded theater when there was no fire, your right to free speech would not be protected by the 1st

Amendment. The court has determined that no one has the right to endanger others just because he or she has the right to speak freely.

"If enough openings become available in the Supreme Court during a president's term he can influence or totally change the political posture of the court. Because these appointments are for life, the justices can affect the nature of Supreme Court rulings for decades to come. If a president is able to fill a seat on the Supreme Court with someone who thinks like he and his party do, the opposing party may not find future Supreme Court rulings much to their liking.

"Our last president, Ronald Reagan, found himself in just such a position," explained Maria. "Through his successful appointments, he effectively caused the political position of the court to shift dramatically in favor of his party, the conservative Republican Party."

Democrats in the Senate, led by Senator Ted Kennedy of Massachusetts, fought hard to prevent the appointment of Reagan's choices, fearing a reversal of many political gains made by the Democratic party over the last 30 years. Although the Democrats successfully blocked the appointment of two Reagan candidates, the result was still a shift in political views of the Supreme Court as a whole.

The sensitive political nature of these Supreme Court appointments have resulted in at least 13 Congressional resolutions to change the way justices are chosen. Yet the process remains relatively unchanged.

Other Duties

Maria summed up the subject of the presidency. "The duties of the president are clearly stated in the Constitution." She read directly from the document: "He (the president) shall from time to time give to the Congress information of the state of the Union." Maria looked at the class.

"Can anyone tell me what this means?"

"Does it mean that the president has to deliver the 'State of the Union' address to Congress each year?" asked Henri.

"Yes and no," Maria replied. "The truth is that presidents have often been reluctant to communicate with Congress. From John

Adams to Woodrow Wilson, not one president wanted to make an appearance before a meeting of the Congress. Today's custom of the State of the Union address began in modern times following Woodrow Wilson's example.

"The president may also recommend bills to be considered before the Congress. This is another way a bill can be presented to Congress and eventually become law.

"And he can also 'on extraordinary occasions' call for a special session of either or both houses of Congress whenever he feels the issues require this action. Or, to quote the Constitution, 'to such times as he may think proper.'"

"Finally, the president may 'receive ambassadors and other public ministers,' which tells us why the State Department was created. And he shall 'take care that the laws be faithfully executed.' This last clause establishes the president's authority as chief law enforcement officer."

Implied Powers

Maria offered a few words of encouragement. "I know this has been a long evening, but there is just one more area I must touch on briefly before we can all go home. So far I've told you about what are called the president's express powers, or powers specifically listed in the Constitution. But of equal importance are his 'implied' powers. The question is, are they the implied powers of the office or the person?

"An example of this is the president's power to wage war as commander in chief of the armed forces. Even though the Congress holds sole power to declare war, American presidents have committed troops to combat many times throughout our history, while Congress has only declared war only five times. Congress tried to curtail this power with the War Powers Act in 1973, but the president still has implied powers to commit to an armed struggle prior to advising the Congress.

"Another good example is that as chief legislator, the president influences new laws by constitutional right according to the political force of his personality.

"Look at the early days of Ronald Reagan's presidency. His enormous popularity had a great effect on opposition congressional members seeking reelection. This is where a popular president can accomplish a lot more than an unpopular one.

"We have to remember, however, that the judiciary—our court system—keeps a watchful eye on both the president and the Congress. In many ways, the judiciary has had as much to do with shaping our country today as the other two branches. And that's what checks and balances are all about."

And with just a hint of things to come, Maria thanked her students for being so attentive, picked up her briefcase, and followed everyone out the door.

6

The Branch Of The Judiciary

"**T**he United States has a kind of continuing constitutional convention," said Maria at the start of their next class. "It's called the Supreme Court, and it and a number of lower courts were created by Article III of the Constitution."

"I do not understand," Mohammed spoke up, "either something is constitutional or it is not, right?"

"Time," Maria explained, "has its effect on all things. We grow old and die. Also, as we grow older, our views on life are different, right?" Maria looked with satisfaction upon the room of nodding heads.

"Well, the same is true with a country. Cultures change, and people's attitudes toward social issues are different. For example, one of the most infamous decisions of the Supreme Court occurred in 1857. It was called *Dred Scott versus Sandford*. The court ruled that 'separate but equal' accommodations for the races was constitutional. At that time, this act virtually denied that black people were citizens of the United States, even though they lived in a supposedly 'free' state.

"This sounds awful to us now. But it's important," Maria emphasized, "to understand that the government is made up of people like you and me who respond to their individual feelings and prejudices. The Supreme Court is human too. So their decisions often reflect 'acceptable' social values of the day. What would be unthinkable

The United States Supreme Court—the highest court in the judiciary branch of government—meets in this elegant building in Washington, D.C.

today was, for the most part, routine in the early 1800s. Hence, the Dred Scott decision continued to legitimize human slavery. It took the Civil War and President Lincoln to change that."

Maria asked Canadian-born Julia Manfred to give her oral report about the most significant Supreme Court case in American race relations since Dred Scott. Julia shyly approached the front of the room, note cards in hand. She looked a bit nervous, but soon launched into a good summary of *Brown versus Board of Education.*

"The Court ruled that 'equal protection' under the law included education, and went one logical step further by outlawing segregation altogether. This revolutionary decision not only affected black people, but anyone who may have cause to feel discriminated against."

"Many Americans believed then and still believe now that the Supreme Court was 'legislating' through such decisions, and taking an 'activist' role in government," said Maria. "Do you think that's good or bad?"

"Isn't that what checks and balances are all about?" responded Julia. "If Congress or the president gets upset over a Supreme Court decision, they can try to get around it by passing a new law or constitutional amendment."

Dolores spoke up. "That's what they tried to do with the 'flag burning' issue. Congress tried to pass a constitutional amendment banning flag desecration. But they couldn't get the votes. Too many felt that burning the flag is protected by the 1st Amendment."

Maria was pleased that her students were becoming such quick studies. She talked a little more about the court system and discrimination. The drive for equality continued through legislative efforts. Affirmative action programs that mandated quotas for employment and education were enacted. These actions brought to the courts a new term—"reverse discrimination."

In the Bakke case, the courts found that a medical school admissions program established at a California college campus was unfair to whites in favor of minorities because it enforced a quota system. This decision shows how the courts are sensitive to sentiments of the day.

Supreme Court rulings affect how the government does business as well. One of the most noted was *Marbury versus Marbury* (1803), where Chief Justice John Marshall "declared" that the court had the power of "judicial review," and could decide what the Constitution meant and find a law or action either constitutional or unconstitutional.

This is an important case because Article III of the Constitution only defines the courts in general, the types of cases it may try, and the jurisdiction of the courts regarding federal and state issues. It does not, however, say that the court interprets the Constitution and can judge the validity of a given law.

In the natural struggle for power which occurs between the three branches of government, Chief Justice Marshall simply declared that the Supreme Court will have the last word. Yet in practice, any ruling of the Supreme Court must stand not only the test of time, but the attitudes and beliefs of the people.

"And it remains true to this day," said Maria.

With a few exceptions, lower courts must first try a case before the Supreme Court will consider whether to review a case on appeal. Today thousands of requests are made to the Supreme Court every year to hear a case. Barely 200 receive a hearing. The justices only have so much time, so they must pick and choose the cases they'll accept. When they refuse to hear a case, that means the lower court ruling stands.

"Speaking of cases," said Maria. "do you know what crime is the only one mentioned in the Constitution?"

"Long-winded speeches?" suggested Emilio.

"No!" laughed Maria. "It's treason. Treason against the United States means giving aid and comfort to our enemies. I'm sure some of you have heard about Aaron Burr."

Burr, a former vice president, was the first high official to be charged with treason in 1807. He was acquitted because President Thomas Jefferson's prosecutors could not prove the charge. Since then, many cases have been tried. The most famous one in recent times involved the Walker family, where a father and son sold U.S. Navy secrets to the Soviet Union.

Punishment for treason is decided by Congress. The Constitution forbids, however, "corruption of blood," a phrase meaning children or family should not be affected by the conduct of the convicted person (which has been common in other forms of government).

Maria paused for a moment. "There is one thing we should not overlook. Notice how the Constitution gives no power to the courts to enforce their decisions. Instead, the courts must rely on the other two branches— the holders of 'the purse and the sword'—to enforce them. In other words, we have no secret police to carry out the courts' agenda. It's another example of checks and balances."

"Why are there nine Supreme Court justices?" asked Juanita.

"Actually, there is no reason. Nothing is said in the Constitution about the size of the Supreme Court. Modern tradition established nine as the

Affecting the Federal System:

McCULLOCH V. MARYLAND (1819) - The national government is supreme within its sphere of authority and has a wide choice of means to implement its constitutional powers.

COHENS V. VIRGINIA (1821) - The Supreme Court has jurisdiction over the state courts in constitutional matters.

Affecting the Separation of Powers:

HUMPHREY'S EXECUTOR V. UNITED STATES (1935) - The president's power to remove executive officials does not extend to independent agencies.

YOUNGSTOWN SHEET AND TUBE CO. V. SAWER (1952) - The president may not seize private property without congressional authorization.

WATKINS V. UNITED STATES (1957) - There are limitations on the power of Congress to investigate.

UNITED STATES V. NIXON (1974) - The executive's privilege to withhold information is not absolute.

Affecting Foreign Affairs and National Security:

MISSOURI V. HOLLAND (1920) - The treaty-making power of Congress has supremacy over the states.

UNITED STATES V. CURTISS-WRIGHT EXPORT CORP. (1936) - In the field of foreign policy, Congress has the power to delegate broad authority to the president.

UNITED STATES V. BELMONT (1937) - Executive agreements, like treaties, supersede state law.

KOREMATSU V. UNITED STATES (1944) - The circumstances of war may justify the detention of American citizens.

Affecting Due Process:

ROE V. WADE (1973) - The right to an abortion is guaranteed by the Constitution's "right of privacy."

Affecting Equal Protection:

PLESSY V. FERGUSON (1896) - The Court sanctions "separate but equal" accommodations for the races.

BROWN V. BOARD OF EDUCATION OF TOPEKA (1954) - Segregation on the basis of race is a denial of equal protection in violation of the Constitution.

ABINGTON SCHOOL DISTRICT V. SCHEMPP (1963) - State and local rules requiring prayers or other religious exercises in public schools violate the First Amendment.

REGENTS OF THE UNIVERSITY OF CALIFORNIA V. REGENTS BAKKE (1978) - Preferential racial quotas in education violate the Civil Rights Act of 1964.

number, but there have been as many as ten and as few as six.

"In fact, the office of Chief Justice is considered by many to be more powerful than that of the president. To date we've had 16 chief justices and 103 justices. Twenty-four candidates for justice were rejected by the Senate. One former president, William Taft, became the tenth chief justice, and one justice, Charles Hughs, resigned to run for president. He eventually was appointed to the office of chief justice by President Herbert Hoover.

"But who's counting?" Maria said. "Let's go home."

7

The States And The Federal Government

Maria decided to add some human interest to her class by relating something they could all understand to an important part of their discussion of the Constitution.

"Let me describe the relationship between state and federal government this way: it's like the relationship a family has to its community. In your families you probably have house rules, chores, and boundaries. Those of you who are parents, you know what I'm talking about. Your home is like your state, and the family next door might not do things exactly the way you do, but they do a lot of similar things like take out the trash, cook meals, and do the laundry.

"But there are other things in which you all cooperate like obeying the laws about not littering and obeying traffic signals. You accept authority in your community regarding some matters."

Maria then pointed out that the states have much the same relationship with the federal government. For example, Article IV defines the "intrastate" privileges and immunities of state citizens, offers certain guarantees to the states, and defines the rights reserved to the states.

One of these rights is called the "friendship clause": Full faith and credit shall be given to each state to the public acts, records, and judicial proceedings of every other state. This means that state and federal governments collectively recognize one another's contracts, wills, and civil judgments.

Section 2 of this article states that the citizens of each state shall have the privileges and immunities of the citizens of every other state. For example, a citizen may travel from state to state, or do business in a neighboring state, and expect to be treated the same as a citizen of that state. If you commit a crime in one state and cross the border to another, the governor of the first state can demand your return.

"I don't understand," said Julia. "Are you saying that if I commit a crime in New York and drive to New Jersey, I must be turned over to New York if the governor demands it?"

"Yes," replied Maria, "but New York first has to ask for your return. 'Extradition,' as the process is called, is not really automatic."

In the early history of our country, extradition was often ignored in favor of protecting a local citizen. Prior to the Civil War, border states often looked the other way as citizens from both the north and south "raided" neighboring states and fled to the safety of home. Today, extradition is taken for granted as an accepted legal practice.

Another clause was written specifically for the extradition of runaway slaves—that is, to allow the recapture of fugitive slaves. This clause had a tragic effect. One Chief Justice, Roger Taney, declared in the Dred Scott case that blacks were not people but "articles of merchandise." This decision was just one of many that made the Civil War all but inevitable. This "fugitive slave clause" was not part of the Articles of Confederation, but was a southern proposal which in effect turned slavery into a national institution protected by federal law. It was later changed by the 13th Amendment.

Article IV also defines the requirements of admission of new states and the power of Congress over territory and property. This section protects the existing states, but only if they want protection. For example, if Connecticut, Rhode Island and Massachusetts wanted to merge —that is, combine into one big state—the Constitution would not prohibit the move if each state legislature and the Congress all agreed.

"I've heard some people want to divide northern and southern California into two separate states," said Karl. "Is that possible?"

"Sure," said Maria. "Again, as long as all the parties agree. But the Congress also has the power to dispose of and make all rules concern-

Dr. Martin Luther King, Jr., led the fight for civil rights in the 1950s and '60s, demanding equality of treatment in all areas of American life as guaranteed by the Constitution.

ing territory and property owned by the United States."

"So Congress is like a property manager or landlord," said Robert.

"Good," Maria agreed. "In all territorial matters, the Congress would be consulted and expected to manage the territory. The Constitution adds, 'nothing in this Constitution shall be so construed as to prejudice any claims of the United States, or any particular state.'

"What this means is that any dispute over territory by either the United States or an individual state will be heard by the Congress without any prejudgment. This is really not so important to us now, but when people were just starting to move west, no one knew how many states would be added.

"There is also a clause that guarantees that the federal government shall protect every state from foreign invasion, and also from domestic rioting that threatens a state government.

"But states cannot set up a monarchy. A state can't decide to have a king, for example. The federal government will only tolerate a representative form of government. In the Constitution this is what is meant by the word 'republican.'

Methods Of Amendment

Maria saw a questioning look on Emilio's face. "Señora Chase, this is interesting, but the Constitution is over 200 years old. But you have talked about 'amending' the Constitution. How does that happen?"

"If public opinion disagrees with the Constitution as it is today," Maria answered, "we can change it in several ways.

"The framers of the Constitution understood that the new nation they had created was a nation of individuals. Having lived under the trying times necessary to change their government, they were naturally concerned with someday having to do it all over again. They knew people and societies change—again, this was true of their own situation. The government they had created must respond to the will of the people, not the other way around.

"With this in mind, the framers invented the amendment process so that the people could revise their government in a peaceful, orderly

Failed Amendments

Over 10,000 amendments to the Constitution have been proposed to Congress since ratification. Of these, 26 became part of the Constitution. Seven of those 10,000 that made it to the ratification vote, yet failed, were:

1789   Ratio of House membership to population.

1789   Compensation of members of Congress.

1810   Abrogation (surrender) of American citizenship for accepting gifts or titles of nobility from a foreign government without the consent of Congress. This amendment missed by one vote.

1861   Non-Congressional interference in slavery. Offered to head off the Civil War, it was adopted by only two states. President Lincoln signed the ratified 13th Amendment which in effect neutralized any further effort to support slavery.

1924   Prohibition of labor of persons under 18 years of age. Opposed by manufacturing associations and some religious groups.

1972   ERA. The Equal Rights Amendment; equality of rights cannot be denied because of gender. Failed at best by three votes, has more or less faded as interest dropped off.

1978   Representation of the District of Columbia in the House and the Senate. The District of Columbia has a population higher than four states, but it failed anyway.

Some new proposals for amendments that have been seriously discussed in the 1980s and 1990s are:

- A "balanced budget" amendment, to force the federal government to spend only as much as it collects in taxes and other revenues.

- A four-year term for representatives in Congress.

- Limiting all members of Congress to two terms, like the president.

- The "Line Item Veto," allowing the president to veto single items within a bill instead of vetoing an entire bill, as now required.

- A modification of the treaty-making process between the United States and foreign countries.

fashion. Article V of the Constitution defines the amendment method." Maria handed out printed copies of the following:

> 1. Congress proposes the new amendment by a vote of two-thirds of both houses. Next, the new amendment must be ratified by three-fourths of the state legislatures. The Constitution now has a new amendment.
>
> 2. Congress proposes a new amendment by a two-thirds vote in both houses, then calls for a special ratifying convention to be held in three-fourths of the states in the Union. Once ratified, the Constitution has a new amendment.
>
> 3. A national convention is called by Congress after a request by two-thirds of the state legislatures, where the amendment or amendments are proposed and then ratified by three-fourths of the state legislatures.
>
> 4. A national convention is called by Congress after a request by two-thirds of the state legislatures in the Union. Then a special ratifying convention is held in three-fourths of the states in the Union. Once ratified, the constitution has a new amendment.

Maria grinned. "I know what you're all thinking. You think they all say the same thing four times. But they're all a little different."

Maria then explained that the Constitution provides four separate methods to be sure that no single political path may be blocked by determined opponents to change. For instance, in the first approach,

Congress proposes the new amendment that the state legislatures must ratify or reject. In the second approach, the state legislature is bypassed by a special convention that requires delegates to attend from each state, yet the new amendment is still proposed by Congress.

The next two ways are basically the same, except that the states request the amendment and the legislature ratifies it, or the states request a vote and a special state convention ratifies the measure. The national convention is called by Congress only after the states request that a new amendment be considered.

With that, the clock showed it was time for a coffee break. "Just in time too," thought Maria. "That explanation always needs time to sink in."

8

The Price Of Freedom

"**W**ell, class, it's almost over. All we have left to discuss are the 'general provisions' in the Constitution," said Maria.

"You mean the loose ends," joked Henri, sitting way in the back.

"That's right, Henri, a place for the odds and ends—just like the back of the classroom," Maria replied with a grin. "But I don't want you to think the general provisions are any less important because of where they appear in the document.

"For example, one paragraph establishes the supremacy of the Constitution as our law. 'This Constitution…shall be the supreme law of the land,' it says. What do you suppose that means, Juanita?"

"That no other law is any higher?"

"Correct," said Maria. "To the lawmakers of the Congress and the state legislatures, this is probably the most important clause in the Constitution. And the founders wrote it so that nothing can be assumed or taken for granted. By establishing the Constitution as 'supreme law,' no new laws—local or state—can be contrary to or disagree with the Constitution.

"I'll give you just one example where this principle was tested: the Civil War. There's nothing in our Constitution about the right of states to secede, or leave the United States for good. When the Confederacy was formed and declared its separation from the Union in 1861, the war was on. The results of this one decision were tragic: the Civil War took more lives than any other American conflict except World War II."

Oaths

Maria then discussed another general provision: an Oath of Office required by all representatives to uphold the Constitution. It specifically prohibits any religious test as a qualification to hold office.

The fact that no religious test is required under the Constitution was unanimously passed by the delegates at the Constitutional Convention, even though 11 of the 13 states had religious qualifications of their own for state representatives. Upon ratification of the Constitution, each of those states had to strike their laws mandating religious tests. Nowhere does the Constitution address the separation of church and state, however, and God is not mentioned once (but it is mentioned in the Declaration of Independence).

"Why were they so anti-religion?" asked Miyoshi.

"They weren't really," Maria said. "They debated about this quite a bit. In fact, as a group these men were probably very much in favor of religious influence in public life. But they remembered too well that the country was founded by many who had escaped religious persecution in Europe. These people wanted religious freedom, and so by carefully removing any religious language from the Constitution, the framers were declaring that religion and government are two separate issues. Religion may influence the individual, of course, and the individual may influence government, but no one can use the Constitution to force religious beliefs on other citizens.

"As for requiring an oath to 'support this Constitution,' it may seem unnecessary, but it was included because it reinforces the 'supreme law of the land' clause. Eighty-seven years later, many people still felt more loyalty to their own state than to the United States. The Civil War was evidence of this.

"Take General Robert E. Lee, for example. He was against seces-

The Eighth Amendment to the Constitution forbids "cruel and unusual punishment." Although many Americans believe capital punishment fits this definition, the Supreme Court ruled in 1976 that the death penalty did not violate the Constitution.

sion and slavery, yet he felt he had to defend his home state of Virginia. Many northern officers felt secession was strictly a state issue and they were indifferent to slavery, yet they chose to fight for the Union.

"It seems a bit messy to cram all of these different issues and instructions and rules into just seven articles," said Evita. "Couldn't they have made it a little easier to follow?"

"Good point," Maria laughed. "As a matter of fact, during the constitutional convention there were 23 articles to consider. A committee headed by Governor Morris of Pennsylvania condensed these articles into only seven. The seventh article is the only one that has no relevance to today's government. It simply contained the rules for ratifying the Constitution. Nine states had to vote yes."

Ratification

The Constitution was ratified when New Hampshire approved the document on June 21, 1788. The new government met with eight of 22 senators and 13 of 59 representatives present on March 4, 1789.

On April 30, 1789, George Washington was sworn in as chief executive in the nation's capitol at that time, New York City. On September 24, 1789, the New Federal Congress passed the Judiciary Act of 1789 that established a Supreme Court, 13 district courts, and three circuit (traveling) courts.

The next day, September 25, Congress submitted 12 amendments to the two-year-old Constitution to the states for approval. Two of these, an amendment concerning the ratio of members in the House of Representatives to state population, and an amendment controlling the compensation of members of Congress, failed to pass. The remaining ten are known as the Bill of Rights.

The new government took hold, and the new Constitution began to fulfill its promise.

Citizen Constituents

Maria was satisfied that her students would leave her class with at least an understanding of how important the Constitution was to their lives as Americans and, she hoped, they would feel proud of what they were working to become: American citizens.

"I have just one more question for you," she said. "Can anyone tell me what is the price of freedom?"

The room was absolutely quiet. Maria smiled. "That's okay, this is sort of a trick question—but a very important one.

"The price of freedom is a difficult concept to understand. As Americans, we have been showered with patriotic sayings such as 'eternal vigilance is the price of freedom,' or 'thousands of Americans

"Congress shall make no law respecting an establishment of religion, or prohibiting the free exercise thereof...." These were the first words in the first article in the Bill of Rights. More than 200 years later, Americans are still free to worship—or not worship—in any way they choose.

have died for your freedom.' Both of these statements are true. But you may ask, 'what does this have to do with me?'

"The Constitution of the United States was born in stormy times, when emotions of discontent ran high. Many early Americans were not happy with what was happening in their lives, and they decided to do something about it. Since then, Americans continue to speak up about things that bother them.

"In the more than 200 years we have existed as a nation, nearly 10,000 amendments have been submitted to the Congress for consideration. Think what that means. It means that people were discontented enough over so many issues that they found the time to participate in government. Some of these proposed changes to the Constitution may have been misguided, but they demonstrated that we truly have a government 'by the people.'

"Each of those 10,000 amendments had someone like you and me—an American willing to take the issue to the people for acceptance or rejection—behind it. They all paid a small part of the price of freedom.

"And that small price is the participation, the active, thoughtful effort of the 'citizen constituent.' You are becoming a part of this now. You're inheriting a great tradition. What the founders did then will benefit you now. Does everyone understand?"

They did.

Appendix

FEDERAL CONSTITUTION

Preamble

We the People of the United States, in Order to form a more perfect Union, establish Justice, insure domestic Tranquility, provide for the common defence, promote the general Welfare, and secure the Blessings of Liberty to ourselves and our Posterity, do ordain and establish this Constitution for the United States of America.

Article I

Section 1. All legislative Powers herein granted shall be vested in a Congress of the United States, which shall consist of a Senate and House of Representatives.

Section 2. The House of Representatives shall be composed of Members chosen every second Year by the people of the several States, and the Electors in each State shall have the Qualifications requisite for Electors of the most numerous Branch of the State Legislature.

No Person shall be a Representative who shall not have attained to the Age of twenty five Years, and been seven Years a Citizen of the United States, and who shall not, when elected, be an inhabitant of that State in which he shall be chosen.

Representatives and direct Taxes shall be apportioned among the several States which may be included within this Union, according to their respective Numbers, [which shall be determined by adding to the whole Number of free Persons, including those bound to Service for a Term of Years, and excluding Indians not taxed, three fifths of all other persons.][1] The actual Enumeration shall be made within three Years after the first Meeting of the Congress of the United States, and within every subsequent Term of ten

[1] Superseded by the Fourteenth Amendment.

Years, in such Manner as they shall by Law direct. The Number of Representatives shall not exceed one for every thirty Thousand, but each State shall have at Least one Representative; and until such enumeration shall be made, the State of New Hampshire shall be entitled to chuse three, Massachusetts eight, Rhode-Island and Providence Plantations one, Connecticut five, New-York six, New Jersey four, Pennsylvania eight, Delaware one, Maryland six, Virginia ten, North Carolina five, South Carolina five, and Georgia three.

When vacancies happen in the Representation from any State, the Executive Authority thereof shall issue Writs of Election to fill such Vacancies.

The House of Representatives shall chuse their Speaker and other Officers; and shall have the sole Power of Impeachment.

Section 3. The Senate of the United States shall be composed of two Senators from each State, [chosen by the Legislature thereof,]^2 for six Years; and each Senator shall have one Vote.

Immediately after they shall be assembled in Consequence of the first Election, they shall be divided as equally as may be into three Classes. The Seats of the Senators of the first Class shall be vacated at the Expiration of the second Year, of the second Class at the Expiration of the fourth Year, and of the third Class at the Expiration of the sixth Year, so that one third may be chosen every second Year; [and if Vacancies happen by Resignation, or otherwise, during the Recess of the Legislature of any State, the Executive thereof may make temporary Appointments until the next Meeting of the Legislature, which shall then fill such Vacancies.]^3

No Person shall be a Senator who shall not have attained to the Age of thirty Years, and been nine Years a Citizen of the United States, and who shall not, when elected, be an inhabitant of that State for which he shall be chosen.

The Vice President of the United States shall be President of the Senate,

---

2 Superseded by the Seventeenth Amendment.
3 Modified by the Seventeenth Amendment.

but shall have no Vote, unless they be equally divided.

The Senate shall chuse their other Officers, and also a President pro tempore, in the Absence of the Vice President, or when he shall exercise the Office of President of the United States.

The Senate shall have the sole Power to try all Impeachments. When sitting for that Purpose, they shall be on Oath or Affirmation. When the President of the United States is tried, the Chief Justice shall preside: and no Person shall be convicted without the Concurrence of two thirds of the Members present.

Judgment in Cases of Impeachment shall not extend further than to removal from Office, and disqualification to hold and enjoy any Office of honor, Trust or Profit under the United States: but the Party convicted shall nevertheless be liable and subject to Indictment, Trial, Judgment and Punishment, according to Law.

Section 4. The Times, Place and Manner of holding Elections for Senators and Representatives shall be prescribed in each State by the Legislature thereof; but the Congress may at any time by Law make or alter such Regulations, except as to the Places of chusing Senators.

[The Congress shall assemble at least once in every Year, and such Meeting shall be on the first Monday in December, unless they shall by Law appoint a different Day.][4]

Section 5. Each House shall be the Judge of the Elections, Returns and Qualifications of its own Members, and a Majority of each shall constitute a Quorum to do Business; but a smaller Number may adjourn from day to day, and may be authorized to compel the Attendance of absent Members, in such Manner, and under such Penalties as each House may provide.

Each House may determine the Rules of its Proceedings, punish its Members for disorderly Behaviour, and, with the Concurrence of two thirds, expel a Member.

---

[4] Superseded by the Twentieth Amendment.

Each House shall keep a Journal of its Proceedings, and from time to time publish the same, excepting such Parts as may in their Judgment require Secrecy; and the Yeas and Nays of the Members of either House on any question shall, at the Desire of one fifth of those Present, be entered on the Journal.

Neither House, during the Session of Congress, shall, without the Consent of the other, adjourn for more than three days, nor to any other Place than that in which the two Houses shall be sitting.

Section 6. The Senators and Representatives shall receive a Compensation for their Services, to be ascertained by Law, and paid out of the Treasury of the United States. They shall in all Cases, except Treason, Felony and Breach of the Peace, be privileged from Arrest during their Attendance at the Session of their respective Houses, and in going to and returning from the same; and for any Speech or Debate in either House, they shall not be questioned in any other Place.

No Senator or Representative shall, during the Time for which he was elected, be appointed to any civil Office under the Authority of the United States, which shall have been created, or the Emoluments whereof shall have been encreased during such time; and no Person holding any Office under the United States, shall be a Member of either House during his Continuance in Office.

Section 7. All bills for raising Revenue shall originate in the House of Representatives; but the Senate may propose or concur with Amendments as on other Bills.

Every Bill which shall have passed the House of Representatives and the Senate, shall, before it become a Law, be presented to the President of the United States. If he approve he shall sign it, but if not he shall return it, with his Objections to that House in which it shall have originated, who shall enter the Objections at large on their Journal, and proceed to reconsider it. If after such Reconsideration two thirds of that House shall agree to pass the Bill, it shall be sent, together with the Objections, to the other House, by which it shall likewise be reconsidered, and if approved by two thirds of that House, it shall become a Law. But in all such cases the Votes of both Houses shall be determined by Yeas and Nays, and the Names of the Persons voting for and against the Bill shall be entered on the Journal of each House respectively. If any Bill shall not be returned by the President within ten Days (Sundays excepted) after it shall have been presented to him, the Same shall be a Law, in like Manner as if he had signed it, unless the Congress by their Adjournment prevent its Return, in which Case it shall not be a Law.

Every Order, Resolution or Vote to which the Concurrence of the Senate and House of Representatives may be necessary (except on a question of Adjournment) shall be presented to the President of the United States; and before the Same shall take Effect, shall be approved by him, or being disapproved by him, shall be repassed by two thirds of the Senate and House of Representatives, according to the Rules and Limitations prescribed in the Case of a Bill.

Section 8. The Congress shall have Power To lay and collect Taxes, Duties, Imposts and Excises, to pay the Debts and provide for the common Defence and general Welfare of the United States; but all Duties, Imposts and Excises shall be uniform throughout the United States;

To borrow Money on the credit of the United States;

To regulate Commerce with foreign Nations, and among the several States, and with the Indian Tribes;

To establish an uniform Rule of Naturalization, and uniform Laws on the subject of Bankruptcies throughout the United States;

To coin Money, regulate the Value thereof, and of foreign Coin, and fix the Standard of Weights and Measures;

To provide for the Punishment of counterfeiting the Securities and current Coin of the United States;

To establish Post Offices and post Roads;

To promote the Progress of Science and useful Arts, by securing for limited Times to Authors and Inventors the exclusive Right to their respective

Writings and Discoveries;

To constitute Tribunals inferior to the supreme Court;

To define and punish Piracies and Felonies committed on the high Seas, and Offences against the Law of Nations;

To declare War, grant Letters of Marque and Reprisal, and make Rules concerning Captures on Land and Water;

To raise and support Armies, but no Appropriation of Money to that Use shall be for a longer Term than two Years;

To provide and maintain a Navy;

To make Rules for the Government and Regulation of the land and naval Forces;

To provide for calling forth the Militia to execute the Laws of the Union, suppress Insurrections and repel Invasions;

To provide for organizing, arming, and disciplining, the Militia, and for governing such Part of them as may be employed in the Service of the United States, reserving to the States respectively, the Appointment of the Officers, and the Authority of training the Militia according to the discipline prescribed by Congress;

To exercise exclusive Legislation in all Cases whatsoever, over such District (not exceeding ten Miles square) as may, by Cession of particular States, and the Acceptance of Congress, become the Seat of the Government of the United States, and to exercise like Authority over all Places purchased by the Consent of the Legislature of the State in which the Same shall be, for the Erection of Forts, Magazines, Arsenals, dock-Yards, and other needful Buildings;—And

To make all Laws which shall be necessary and proper for carrying into Execution the foregoing Powers, and all other Powers vested by this Constitution in the Government of the United States, or in any Department or Officer thereof.

Section 9. The Migration or Importation of such Persons as any of the States now existing shall think proper to admit, shall not be prohibited by the Congress prior to the Year one thousand eight hundred and eight, but a Tax or duty may be imposed on such Importation, not exceeding ten dollars for each Person.

The Privilege of the Writ of Habeas Corpus shall not be suspended, unless when in Cases of Rebellion or Invasion the public safety may require it.

No Bill of Attainder or ex post facto Law shall be passed.

No Capitation, or other direct, Tax shall be laid, unless in Proportion to the Census or Enumeration herein before directed to be taken.[5]

No Tax or Duty shall be laid on Articles exported from any State.

No Preference shall be given by any Regulation of Commerce or Revenue to the Ports of one State over those of another; nor shall Vessels bound to, or from, one State, be obliged to enter, clear, or pay Duties in another.

No money shall be drawn from the Treasury, but in Consequence of Appropriations made by Law; and a regular Statement and Account of the Receipts and Expenditures of all public Money shall be published from time to time.

No Title of Nobility shall be granted by the United States: And no Person holding any Office of Profit or Trust under them, shall, without the Consent of the Congress, accept of any present, Emolument, Office, or Title, of any kind whatever, from any King, Prince, or foreign State.

Section 10. No State shall enter into any Treaty, Alliance, or Confederation; grant Letters of Marque and Reprisal; coin Money; emit

---

[5] Modified by the Sixteenth Amendment.

Bills of Credit; make any Thing but gold and silver Coin a Tender in Payment of Debts; pass any Bill of Attainder; ex post facto Law, or Law impairing the Obligation of Contracts, or grant any Title of Nobility.

No State shall, without the Consent of the Congress, lay any Imposts or Duties on Imports or Exports, except what may be absolutely necessary for executing it's inspection laws; and the net Product of all Duties and Imposts, laid by any State on Imports or Exports, shall be for the Use of the Treasury of the United States; and all such Laws shall be subject to the Revision and Controul of the Congress.

No State shall, without the Consent of Congress, lay any Duty of Tonnage, keep Troops, or Ships of War in time of Peace, enter into any Agreement or Compact with another State, or with a foreign Power, or engage in War, unless actually invaded, or in such imminent Danger as well not admit of delay.

Article II

Section 1. The executive Power shall be vested in a President of the United States of America. He shall hold his Office during the Term of four Years, and, together with the Vice President, chosen for the same Term, be elected, as follows

Each State shall appoint, in such Manner as the Legislature thereof may direct, a Number of Electors, equal to the whole Number of Senators and Representatives to which the State may be entitled in the Congress: but no Senator or Representative, or Person holding an Office of Trust or Profit under the United States, shall be appointed an Elector.

[The Electors shall meet in their respective States, and vote by Ballot for two Persons, of whom one at least shall not be an Inhabitant of the same State with themselves. And they shall make a List of all the Persons voted for, and of the Number of Votes for each; which list they shall sign and certify, and transmit sealed to the Seat of the Government of the United States, directed to the President of the Senate. The President of the Senate shall, in the Presence of the Senate and House of Representatives, open all the Certificates, and the Votes shall then be counted. The person having the greatest Number of Votes shall be the President, if such Number be a Majority of the whole Number of Electors appointed; and if there be more than one who have such Majority, and have an equal Number of Votes, then the House of Representatives shall immediately chuse by Ballot one of them for President; and if no Person have a Majority, then from the five highest on the List the said House shall in like Manner chuse the President. But in chusing the President, the Votes shall be taken by States, the Representatives from each State having one Vote; A quorum for this purpose shall consist of a Member or Members from two thirds of the States, and a Majority of all the States shall be necessary to a Choice. In every Case, after the Choice of the President, the Person having the greatest Number of Votes of the Electors shall be the Vice President. But if there should remain two or more who have equal Votes, the Senate shall chuse from them by Ballot the Vice President.][6]

The Congress may determine the Time of chusing the Electors, and the Day on which they shall give their Votes; which Day shall be the same throughout the United States.

No Person except a natural born Citizen, or a Citizen of the United States, at the time of the Adoption of this Constitution, shall be eligible to the Office of President; neither shall any Person be eligible to that Office who shall not have attained to the Age of thirty five Years, and been fourteen Years a Resident within the United States.

In Case of the Removal of the President from Office, or of his Death, Resignation, or Inability to discharge the Powers and Duties of the said Office,[7] the Same shall devolve on the Vice President, and the Congress may by Law provide for the Case of Removal, Death, Resignation or Inability, both of the President and Vice President, declaring what Officer shall then act as President, and such Officer shall act accordingly, until the Disability be removed, or a President shall be elected.

The President shall, at stated Times, receive for his Services, a Compensation, which shall neither be encreased nor diminished during the

[6] Superseded by the Twelfth Amendment.
[7] Modified by the Twenty-fifth Amendment.

Period for which he shall have been elected, and he shall not receive within that Period any other Emolument from the United States, or any of them.

Before he enter on the Execution of his Office, he shall take the following Oath or Affirmation:—"I do solemnly swear (or affirm) that I will faithfully execute the Office of President of the United States, and will to the best of my Ability, preserve, protect and defend the Constitution of the United States."

Section 2. The President shall be Commander in Chief of the Army and Navy of the United States, and of the Militia of the several States, when called into the actual Service of the United States; he may require the Opinion, in writing, of the principal Officer in each of the executive Departments, upon any Subject relating to the Duties of their respective Offices, and he shall have Power to grant Reprieves and Pardons for Offenses against the United States, except in Cases of Impeachment.

He shall have Power, by and with the Advice and Consent of the Senate, to make Treaties, provided two thirds of the Senators present concur; and he shall nominate, and by and with the Advice and Consent of the Senate, shall appoint Ambassadors, other public Ministers and Consuls, Judges of the supreme Court, and all other Officers of the United States, whose Appointments are not herein otherwise provided for, and which shall be established by Law: but the Congress may by Law vest the Appointment of such inferior Officers, as they think proper, in the President alone, in the Courts of Law, or in the Heads of Departments.

The President shall have Power to fill up all Vacancies that may happen during the Recess of the Senate, by granting Commissions which shall expire at the End of their next Session.

Section 3. He shall from time to time give to the Congress Information of the State of the Union, and recommend to their Consideration such Measures as he shall judge necessary and expedient; he may, on extraordinary Occasions, convene both Houses, or either of them, and in Case of Disagreement between them, with Respect to the Time of Adjournment, he may adjourn them to such Time as he shall think proper; he shall receive Ambassadors and other public Ministers; he shall take Care that the Laws be faithfully executed, and shall Commission all Officers of the United States.

Section 4. The President, Vice President and all civil Officers of the United States, shall be removed from Office on Impeachment for, and Conviction of, Treason, Bribery, or other high Crimes and Misdemeanors.

Article III

Section 1. The judicial Power of the United States, shall be vested in one supreme Court, and in such inferior Courts as the Congress may from time to time ordain and establish. The Judges, both of the supreme and inferior Courts, shall hold their Offices during good Behaviour, and shall, at stated Times, receive for their Services, a Compensation, which shall not be diminished during their Continuance in Office.

Section 2. The judicial Power shall extend to all Cases, in Law and Equity, arising under this Constitution, the Laws of the United States, and Treaties made, or which shall be made, under their authority;—to all Cases affecting Ambassadors, other public Ministers and Consuls;—to all Cases of admiralty and maritime Jurisdiction;—to Controversies to which the United States shall be a Party;—to Controversies between two or more States—between a State and Citizens of another State;[8]—between Citizens of different States,—between Citizens of the same State claiming Lands under Grants of different States, and between a State, or the Citizens thereof, and foreign States, Citizens or Subjects.

In all cases affecting Ambassadors, other public Ministers and Consuls, and those in which a State shall be Party, the supreme Court shall have original Jurisdiction. In all the other Cases before mentioned, the supreme Court shall have appellate Jurisdiction, both as to Law and Fact, with such Exceptions, and under such Regulations as the Congress shall make.

The Trial of all Crimes, except in Cases of Impeachment, shall be by Jury; and such Trial shall be held in the State where the said Crimes shall have been committed; but when not committed within any State, the Trial shall be at such Place or Places as the Congress may by law have directed.

Section 3. Treason against the United States, shall consist only in levy-

---

[8] Modified by the Eleventh Amendment.

ing War against them, or in adhering to their Enemies, giving them Aid and Comfort. No Person shall be convicted of Treason unless on the Testimony of two Witnesses to the same overt Act, or on Confession in open Court.

The Congress shall have Power to declare the Punishment of Treason, but no Attainder of Treason shall work Corruption of Blood, or Forfeiture except during the Life of the Person attainted.

Article IV

Section 1. Full Faith and Credit shall be given in each State to the public Acts, Records, and judicial Proceedings of every other State. And the Congress may by general Laws prescribe the Manner in which such Acts, Records and Proceedings shall be proved, and the Effect thereof.

Section 2. The Citizens of each State shall be entitled to all Privileges and Immunities of Citizens in the several States.

A Person charged in any State with Treason, Felony, or other Crime, who shall flee from Justice, and be found in another State, shall on Demand of the executive Authority of the State from which he fled, be delivered up, to be removed to the State having Jurisdiction of the Crime.

[No Person held to Service or Labour in one State, under the Laws thereof, escaping into another, shall, in Consequence of any Law or Regulation therein, be discharged from such Service or Labour, but shall be delivered upon on Claim of the Party to whom such Service or Labour may be due.]9

Section 3. New States may be admitted by the Congress into this Union; but no new State shall be formed or erected within the Jurisdiction of any other State; nor any State be formed by the Junction or two or more States, or Parts of States, without the Consent of the Legislatures of the States concerned as well as of the Congress.

The Congress shall have Power to dispose of and make all needful Rules and Regulations respecting the Territory or other Property belonging to the

---

9 Superseded by the Thirteenth Amendment.

United States; and nothing in this Constitution shall be so construed as to Prejudice any Claims of the United States, or of any particular State.

Section 4. The United States shall guarantee to every State in this Union a Republican Form of Government, and shall protect each of them against Invasion; and on application of the Legislature, or of the Executive (when the Legislature cannot be convened) against domestic Violence.

Article V

The Congress, whenever two thirds of both Houses shall deem it necessary, shall propose Amendments to this Constitution, or, on the Application of the Legislatures of two thirds of the several States, shall call a Convention for proposing Amendments, which, in either Case, shall be valid to all Intents and Purposes, as Part of this Constitution, when ratified by the Legislatures of three fourths of the several States, or by Conventions in three fourths thereof, as the one or the other Mode of Ratification may be proposed by the Congress; Provided that no Amendment which may be made prior to the Year One thousand eight hundred and eight shall in any Manner affect the first and fourth Clauses in the Ninth Section of the first Article; and that no State, without its Consent, shall be deprived of its equal Suffrage in the Senate.

Article VI

All Debts contracted and Engagements entered into, before the Adoption of this Constitution, shall be as valid against the United States under this Constitution, as under the Confederation.

This Constitution, and the Laws of the United States which shall be made in Pursuance thereof; and all Treaties made, or which shall be made, under the Authority of the United States, shall be the supreme Law of the Land; and the Judges in every State shall be bound thereby, any Thing in the Constitution or Laws of any State to the Contrary notwithstanding.

The Senators and Representatives before mentioned, and the Members of the several State Legislatures, and all executive and judicial Officers, both of the United States and of the several States, shall be bound by Oath or Affirmation, to support this Constitution; but no religious Test shall ever be required as a Qualification to any Office or public Trust under the United States.

Article VII

The Ratification of the Conventions of nine States, shall be sufficient for the Establishment of this Constitution between the States so ratifying the Same.

Done in Convention by the Unanimous Consent of the States present the Seventeenth Day of September in the Year of our Lord one thousand seven hundred and Eighty seven and of the Independence of the United States of America the Twelfth.

In witness whereof We have hereunto subscribed our Names.

G. Washington, *President and deputy from Virginia*; *Attest* William Jackson, *Secretary; Delaware*: Geo. Read, Gunning Bedford, Jr., John Dickinson, Richard Bassett, Jaco. Broom; *Maryland*: James McHenry, Daniel of St. Thomas Jenifer, Daniel Carroll; *Virginia*: John Blair, James Madison, Jr.; *North Carolina*: Wm Blount, Richd. Dobbs Spaight, Hu Williamson; *South Carolina*: J. Rutledge, Charles Cotesworth Pinckney, Charles Pinckney, Pierce Butler; *Georgia*: William Few, Abr. Baldwin; *New Hampshire*: John Langdon, Nicholas Gilman; *Massachusetts*: Nathaniel Gorham, Rufus King; *Connecticut:* Wm. Saml. Johnson, Roger Sherman; *New York*: Alexander Hamilton; *New Jersey*: Wil. Livingston, David Brearley, Wm. Paterson, Jona. Dayton; *Pennsylvania:* B. Franklin, Thomas Mifflin, Robt. Morris, Geo. Clymer, Thos. FitzSimons, Jared Ingersoll, James Wilson, Gouv. Morris.

The Bill of Rights [December 15, 1791]

Article I

Congress shall make no law respecting an establishment of religion, or prohibiting the free exercise thereof; or abridging the freedom of speech, or of the press; or the right of the people peaceably to assemble, and to petition the Government for a redress of grievances.

Article II

A well regulated Militia, being necessary to the security of a free State, the right of the people to keep and bear Arms, shall not be infringed.

Article III

No Soldier shall, in time of peace be quartered in any house, without the consent of the Owner, nor in time of war, but in a manner to be prescribed by law.

Article IV

The right of the people to be secure in their persons, houses, papers, and effects, against unreasonable searches and seizures, shall not be violated, and no Warrants shall issue, but upon probable cause, supported by Oath or affirmation, and particularly describing the place to be searched, and the persons or things to be seized.

Article V

No person shall be held to answer for a capital, or otherwise infamous crime, unless on a presentment or indictment of a Grand Jury, except in cases arising in the land or naval forces, or in the Militia, when in actual service in time of War or public danger; nor shall any person be subject for the same offense to be twice put in jeopardy of life or limb; nor shall be compelled in any criminal case to be a witness against himself, nor be deprived of life, liberty, or property, without due process of law; nor shall private property be taken for public use, without just compensation.

Article VI

In all criminal prosecutions, the accused shall enjoy the right to a speedy and public trial, by an impartial jury of the State and district wherein the crime shall have been committed, which district shall have been previously ascertained by law, and to be informed of the nature and cause of the accusation; to be confronted with the witnesses against him; to have compulsory process for obtaining witnesses in his favour, and to have the Assistance of Counsel for his defense.

Article VII

In Suits at common law, where the value in controversy shall exceed twenty dollars, the right of trial by jury shall be preserved, and no fact tried by a jury, shall be otherwise re-examined in any Court of the United States, than according to the rules of the common law.

Article VIII

Excessive bail shall not be required, nor excessive fines imposed, nor cruel and unusual punishments inflicted.

Article IX

The enumeration in the Constitution, of certain rights, shall not be construed to deny or disparage others retained by the people.

Article X

The powers not delegated to the United States by the Constitution, nor prohibited by it to the States, are reserved to the States respectively, or to the people.

Later Amendments

Article XI [January 8, 1798]

The judicial power of the United States shall not be construed to extend to any suit in law or equity, commenced or prosecuted against one of the United States by Citizens of another State, or by Citizens or Subjects of any Foreign State.

Article XII [September 25, 1804]

The Electors shall meet in their respective states, and vote by ballot for

President and Vice-President, one of whom, at least, shall not be an inhabitant of the same state with themselves; they shall name in their ballots the person voted for as President, and in distinct ballots the person voted for as Vice President, and they shall make distinct lists of all persons voted for as President, and of all persons voted for as Vice-President, and of the number of votes for each, which lists they shall sign and certify, and transmit sealed to the seat of the government of the United States, directed to the President of the Senate;—The President of the Senate shall, in the presence of the Senate and House of Representatives, open all the certificates and the votes shall then be counted;—The person having the greatest number of votes for President, shall be the President, if such number be a majority of the whole number of Electors appointed; and if no person have such majority, then from the persons having the highest numbers not exceeding three on the list of those voted for as President, the House of Representatives shall choose immediately, by ballot, the President. But in choosing the President, the votes shall be taken by states, the representation from each state having one vote; a quorum for this purpose shall consist of a member or members from two-thirds of the states, and a majority of all the states shall be necessary to a choice. [And if the House of Representatives shall not choose a President whenever the right of choice shall devolve upon them, before the fourth day of March next following, then the Vice-President shall act as President, as in the case of the death or other constitutional disability of the President.][10] The person having the greatest number of votes as Vice-President, shall be the Vice-President, if such number be a majority of the whole number of Electors appointed, and if no person have a majority, then from the two highest numbers on a list, the Senate shall choose the Vice-President; a quorum for the purpose shall consist of two-thirds of the whole number of Senators, and a majority of the whole number shall be necessary to a choice. But no person constitutionally ineligible to the office of President shall be eligible to that of Vice-President of the United States.

Article XIII [December 18, 1865]

Section 1. Neither slavery nor involuntary servitude, except as a punishment for crime whereof the party shall have been duly convicted, shall exist within the United States, or any place subject to their jurisdiction.

---

[10] Superseded by the Twentieth Amendment.

Section 2. Congress shall have power to enforce this article by appropriate legislation.

Article XIV [July 28, 1868]

Section 1. All persons born or naturalized in the United States, and subject to the jurisdiction thereof, are citizens of the United States and of the State wherein they reside. No State shall make or enforce any law which shall abridge the privileges or immunities of citizens of the United States; nor shall any State deprive any person of life, liberty, or property, without due process of law; nor deny to any person within its jurisdiction the equal protection of the laws.

Section 2. Representatives shall be apportioned among the several States according to their respective numbers, counting the whole number of persons in each State, excluding Indians not taxed. But when the right to vote at any election for the choice of electors for President and Vice President of the United States, Representatives in Congress, the Executive and Judicial officers of a State, or the members of the Legislature thereof, is denied to any of the male inhabitants of such State, being twenty-one years of age, and citizens of the United States, or in any way abridged, except for participation in rebellion, or other crime, the basis of representation therein shall be reduced in the proportion which the number of such male citizens shall bear to the whole number of male citizens twenty-one years of age in such State.

Section 3. No person shall be a Senator or Representative in Congress, or elector of President and Vice President, or hold any office, civil or military, under the United States, or under any State, who, having previously taken an oath, as a member of Congress, or as an officer of the United States, or as a member of any State legislature, or as an executive or judicial officer of any State, to support the Constitution of the United States, shall have engaged in insurrection or rebellion against the same, or given aid and comfort to the enemies thereof. But Congress may by a vote of two-thirds of each House remove such disability.

Section 4. The validity of the public debt of the United States, authorized by law, including debts incurred for payment of pensions and bounties for services in suppressing insurrection or rebellion, shall not be questioned. But neither the United States nor any State shall assume or pay any debt or obligation, incurred in aid of insurrection or rebellion against the United States, or any claim for the loss or emancipation of any slave; but all such debts, obligations and claims shall be held illegal and void.

Section 5. The Congress shall have power to enforce, by appropriate legislation, the provisions of this article.

Article XV [March 30, 1870]

Section 1. The right of citizens of the United States to vote shall not be denied or abridged by the United States or by any State on account of race, color, or previous condition of servitude.

Section 2. The Congress shall have power to enforce this article by appropriate legislation.

Article XVI [February 25, 1913]

The Congress shall have power to lay and collect taxes on incomes, from whatever source derived, without apportionment among the several States, and without regard to any census or enumeration.

Article XVII [May 31, 1913]

The Senate of the United States shall be composed of two Senators from each State, elected by the people thereof, for six years; and each Senator shall have one vote. The electors in each State shall have the qualifications requisite for electors of the most numerous branch of the State legislatures.

When vacancies happen in the representation of any State in the Senate, the executive authority of such State shall issue writs of election to fill such vacancies: *Provided,* That the legislature of any State may empower the executive thereof to make temporary appointments until the people fill the vacancies by election as the legislature may direct.

This amendment shall not be so construed as to affect the election or term of any Senator chosen before it becomes valid as part of the Constitution.

Article XVIII [January 29, 1919]

[*Section 1.* After one year from the ratification of this article the manufacture, sale, or transportation of intoxicating liquors within, the importation thereof into, or the exportation thereof from the United States and all territory subject to the jurisdiction thereof for beverage purposes is hereby prohibited.

Section 2. The Congress and the several States shall have concurrent power to enforce this article by appropriate legislation.

Section 3. This article shall be inoperative unless it shall have been ratified as an amendment to the Constitution by the legislatures of the several States, as provided in the Constitution, within seven years from the date of the submission hereof to the States by the Congress.][11]

Article XIX [August 26, 1920]

The right of citizens of the United States to vote shall not be denied or abridged by the United States or by any State on account of sex.

Congress shall have power to enforce this article by appropriate legislation.

Article XX [February 6, 1933]

Section 1. The terms of the President and Vice President shall end at noon on the 20th day of January, and the terms of Senators and Representatives at noon on the 3d day of January, of the years in which such terms would have ended if this article had not been ratified; and the terms of their successors shall then begin.

Section 2. The Congress shall assemble at least once in every year, and such meeting shall begin at noon on the 3d day of January, unless they shall by law appoint a different day.

Section 3. If, at the time fixed for the beginning of the term of the President, the President elect shall have died, the Vice President elect shall become President. If a President shall not have been chosen before the time fixed for the beginning of his term, or if the President elect shall have failed

---

[11] Superseded by the Twenty-first Amendment.

to qualify, then the Vice President elect shall act as President until a President shall have qualified; and the Congress may by law provide for the case wherein neither a President elect nor a Vice President elect shall have qualified, declaring who shall then act as President, or the manner in which one who is to act shall be selected, and such person shall act accordingly until a President or Vice President shall have qualified.

Section 4. The Congress may by law provide for the case of the death of any of the persons from whom the House of Representatives may choose a President whenever the right of choice shall have devolved upon them, and for the case of the death of any of the persons from whom the Senate may choose a Vice President whenever the right of choice shall have devolved upon them.

Section 5. Sections 1 and 2 shall take effect on the 15th day of October following the ratification of this article.

Section 6. This article shall be inoperative unless it shall have been ratified as an amendment to the Constitution by the legislatures of three-fourths of the several States within seven years from the date of its submission.

Article XXI [December 5, 1933]

Section 1. The eighteenth article of amendment to the Constitution of the United States is hereby repealed.

Section 2. The transportation or importation into any State, Territory, or possession of the United States for delivery to use therein of intoxicating liquors, in violation of the laws thereof, is hereby prohibited.

Section 3. This article shall be inoperative unless it shall have been ratified as an amendment to the Constitution by conventions in the several States, as provided in the Constitution, within seven years from the date of the submission hereof to the States by the Congress.

Article XXII [February 26, 1951]

Section 1. No person shall be elected to the office of the President more than twice, and no person who has held the office of President, or acted as President, for more than two years of a term to which some other person was elected President shall be elected to the office of the President more than once. But this Article shall not apply to any person holding the office of President when this Article was proposed by the Congress, and shall not prevent any person who may be holding the office of President, or acting as President, during the term within which this Article becomes operative from holding the office of President or acting as President during the remainder of such term.

Section 2. This article shall be inoperative unless it shall have been ratified as an amendment to the Constitution by the legislatures of three-fourths of the several States within seven years from the date of its submission to the States by the Congress.

Article XXIII [March 29, 1961]

Section 1. The district constituting the seat of the United States shall appoint in such manner as the Congress may direct:

A number of electors of President and Vice President equal to the whole number of Senators and Representatives in Congress to which the District would be entitled if it were a State, but in no event more than the least populous State; they shall be in addition to those appointed by the States, but they shall be considered, for the purposes of the election of President and Vice President, to be electors appointed by a State; and they shall meet in the District and perform such duties as provided by the twelfth article of amendment.

Section 2. The Congress shall have power to enforce this article by appropriate legislation.

Article XXIV [January 23, 1964]

Section 1. The right of citizens of the United States to vote in any primary or other election for President or Vice President, for electors for President or Vice President, or for Senator or Representative in Congress, shall not be denied or abridged by the United States or any State by reason of failure to pay any poll tax or other tax.

Section 2. The Congress shall have power to enforce this article by appropriate legislation.

Article XXV [February 10, 1967]

Section 1. In case of the removal of the President from office or of his death or resignation, the Vice President shall become President.

Section 2. Whenever there is a vacancy in the office of the Vice President, the President shall nominate a Vice President who shall take office upon confirmation by a majority vote of both Houses of Congress.

Section 3. Whenever the President transmits to the President pro tempore of the Senate and the Speaker of the House of Representatives his written declaration that he is unable to discharge the powers and duties of his office, and until he transmits to them a written declaration to the contrary, such powers and duties shall be discharged by the Vice President as Acting President.

Section 4. Whenever the Vice President and a majority of either the principal officers of the executive departments or of such other body as Congress may by law provide, transmit to the President pro tempore of the Senate and the Speaker of the House of Representatives their written declaration that the President is unable to discharge the powers and duties of his office, the Vice President shall immediately assume the powers and duties of the office as Acting President.

Thereafter, when the President transmits to the President pro tempore of the Senate and the Speaker of the House of Representatives his written declaration that no inability exists, he shall resume the powers and duties of his office unless the Vice President and a majority of either the principal officers of the executive department or of such other body as Congress may by law provide, transmit within four days to the President pro tempore of the Senate and the Speaker of the House of Representatives their written declaration that the President is unable to discharge the powers and duties of his office. Thereupon Congress shall decide the issue, assemblying within forty-eight hours for that purpose if not in session. If the Congress, within twenty-one days after receipt of the latter written declaration, or, if Congress is not in session, within twenty-one days after Congress is required to assemble, determines by two-thirds vote of both Houses that the President is unable to discharge the powers and duties of his office, the Vice President shall continue to discharge the same as Acting President; otherwise, the President shall resume the powers and duties of his office.

Article XXVI [July 1, 1971]

Section 1. The right of citizens of the United States, who are eighteen years of age or older, to vote shall not be denied or abridged by the United States or by any State on account of age.

Section 2. The Congress shall have power to enforce this article by appropriate legislation.

Glossary

AMENDMENT. An article of law added to the Constitution if it is approved (ratified) by a two-thirds majority of the states.

ANTI-FEDERALISTS. Name for the group that opposed ratification of the new Constitution. Patrick Henry was a leading anti-federalist.

ARTICLES OF CONFEDERATION. The document that outlined the first separate American government before the Constitution was written.

BICAMERAL LEGISLATURE. A two-chambered legislative body; Congress is bicameral, with the House of Representatives and Senate.

CONTINENTAL CONGRESS. The first and second colonial assemblies, before the Constitution was written. Delegates came from each colony.

ELECTORAL COLLEGE. The body of electors from each state that meets to officially vote for president and vice president, based upon the popular vote in each state.

EXECUTIVE BRANCH. The branch of government that enforces the law and administers its activities.

FEDERALISTS. Name for the group that supported ratification of the new Constitution. James Madison was a leading federalist.

IMPEACHMENT. The legal process which removes a government official from office.

IMPLIED POWERS. The powers a president may exercise without explicit mention in the Constitution. A strong-willed Congress, or the Supreme Court, may restrict these implied powers.

INALIENABLE RIGHTS. Human rights that all people are born with, that governments cannot restrict.

JUDICIAL BRANCH. The branch of government that interprets the law.

LEGISLATIVE BRANCH. The branch of government that writes the law.

OATH. All elected officials are required to swear or affirm that they will support the Constitution.

PATRIOTS. During the Revolutionary War, these were colonists who sided with the struggle for independence.

RATIFY. When the states approve an amendment to the Constitution.

TORIES. During the Revolutionary War, these were colonists who sided with England against the patriots.

VETO. The president's power to reject a bill that has been passed by Congress.

Bibliography

Landynski. *Living U.S. Constitution*. Mentor Books, 1983

Hamilton, Alexander, et al. *The Federalist Papers*. Mentor Books, 1961

Ketcham. *The Anti-Federalist Papers*. Mentor Books, 1986

Langguth. *Patriots*. Simon and Schuster, 1988

Adler. *We Hold These Truths*. Macmillan, 1987

Bowen. *Miracle At Philadelphia*. Little, Brown & Co., 1986

Lieberman. *The Enduring Constitution*. Harper & Row, 1987

Shafritz. *Dictionary of American Government*. Dorsey, 1988

Index

Picture Credits